◼SCHOLASTIC

Reading Response for Fiction
Graphic Organizers & Mini-Lessons

GRADES 2–4

JENNIFER JACOBSON

New York • Toronto • London • Auckland • Sydney
Mexico City • New Delhi • Hong Kong • Buenos Aires

Teaching
Resources

Introduction

Welcome to *Reading Response for Fiction: Graphic Organizers & Mini-Lessons*! Designed for flexible use, these 20 graphic organizers promote reading response, guiding students to think about and analyze what they read and leading them to read with deeper engagement. By completing the organizers in this book, students receive practice in constructing, examining, and extending meaning; reflecting on the content of text; and refining their reading strategies.

Why Use Graphic Organizers for Reading Response?

Graphic organizers provide schemata: a way of structuring information or arranging key concepts into a pattern, enhancing comprehension and imparting useful learning strategies (Bromley et al., 1995). Organizers offer students an efficient way to direct their attention, record key information, display their thinking, and monitor their use of learning strategies.

Research has shown that graphic organizers help students to:

* connect prior knowledge to new information (Guastello, 2000).

* integrate language and thinking in an organized format (Bromley et al, 1995).

* increase comprehension and retention of text (Boyle & Weishaar, 1997; Chang et al., 2002; Moore & Readence, 1984).

* engage in mid- to high-level thinking along Bloom's Taxonomy (knowledge, comprehension, synthesis, and evaluation) (Dodge, 2005).

The reading response graphic organizers in this book focus on comprehension, reading strategies, story elements, and author's craft. All of the organizers allow students to build upon their prior knowledge, use critical thinking skills, and express what they've learned in their own words.

How to Use This Book

The organizers in this book can be used in any order and lend themselves well to many forms of teaching: pre- and post-assessment, preparation for literature circles, and mini-lessons. They are suitable for use with the whole class, small groups, or individual students, and are ideal for homework or guided cooperative learning groups.

> "The unread story is not a story; it is little black marks on wood pulp. The reader, reading it, makes it live: a live thing, a story."
>
> —Ursula LeGuin

Each organizer targets a different skill or combination of skills, which is shown on each lesson page. At the top of the page, a purpose states the uses and benefits of the activity, and the suggestion for introducing the lesson helps set the stage and pique student interest. Step-by-step directions provide a guide for demonstrating how to use and complete the organizer. Also included is a helpful management tip, which recommends one or more specific ways to use the graphic organizer, and an activity that lets you take students a step further by building on the skills and strategies covered in the lesson or by using the organizer for a different purpose. Finally, to help you get started, books and resources that are referred to in the sample lesson—or that might be appropriate for that particular lesson—are listed in the literature link on the page.

Using a Graphic Organizer

Select the graphic organizer that best suits your instructional needs. Then follow these suggestions to prepare and use the organizer with students.

* **Test It.** Before using an organizer, give it a "trial run" on your own to experience the process firsthand. This will allow you to see how well the graphic works with the selected text. Make any modifications necessary to best meet the needs of your students (Egan, 1999).

* **Present It.** Determine the best method for presenting the graphic organizer. You might make a photocopy for use as a transparency on the overhead projector, or distribute paper copies to students to complete as you model its use. Keep a supply of frequently used organizers on hand for students to use independently.

* **Model It.** Research has shown that graphic organizers are most effective when the teacher presents and models the organizer first for the whole group (Bowman et al., 1998). To ensure greatest success, model the use of each organizer with the whole class before asking students to complete it independently.

Helpful Hints for Success

* You might choose a picture book or familiar fairy tale as your literature selection when introducing a reading response graphic organizer for the first time. With these, you can present an entire story in one lesson, allowing students to focus on the goal and structure of the organizer.

* Introduce the organizer *before* students read. That way, students will read with a strong sense of purpose and focus.

* Model the use of the organizer so that students will gain a clear understanding of its purpose and how to complete it.

* When analyzing text during a mini-lesson, think out loud. This will allow students to recognize and apply your strategies for greater reading comprehension.

* Provide adhesive note strips for students to mark passages that they will later refer to when completing their organizers.

* Urge students not to feel limited by the design of a graphic organizer. Demonstrate writing outside the lines and adding other shapes and lines when making new connections.

* Provide a rich selection of reading materials *and* a variety of reading response graphic organizers to use with them. This will help keep your reading program fresh and interesting.

> As teachers model their own response to literature (through thinking aloud and use of graphic organizers), they make reading strategies explicit. Regular modeling, opportunities to practice and apply the strategies, and consistency in contexts allow students to transfer this knowledge to independent reading and assessment situations (Pardo, 2004).

Assessing Student Performance

Graphic organizers allow you to assess a student's comprehension at a glance. You can use the organizers in this book to determine what students know, the depth of their understanding, what they need to know, what they retain after reading, and the connections they have made. For example, by examining students' responses to Comparing Stories (page 10), you can determine their level of engagement, ability to identify literary elements, and breadth of thinking when making comparisons.

Students can also use graphic organizers to assess their own learning. For example, when completing Book Review Interview (page 36), students may realize they lack sufficient information for summarizing the plot of a story. A motivated learner will go back and reread to fill in the gaps.

Graphic organizers are a performance-based model of assessment and are ideal for including in student portfolios, as they require students to demonstrate both their grasp of the concept and their reasoning.

Connections to the Standards

This book is designed to support you in meeting the following reading standards outlined by Mid-continent Research for Education and Learning (McREL), an organization that collects and synthesizes national and state standards.

Uses the general skills and strategies of the reading process.

* Previews text (e.g. skims materials, uses pictures, textual clues, and text format).

* Understands level-appropriate reading vocabulary (synonyms, antonyms, homophones, multi-meaning words).

* Monitors own reading strategies and makes modifications as needed (recognizes when he or she is confused by a section of text, questions whether the text makes sense).

Uses reading skills and strategies to understand and interpret a variety of literary texts.

* Uses reading skills and strategies to understand a variety of literary passages and texts (fairy tales, folktales, fiction, nonfiction, myths, poems, fables, fantasies, historical fiction, biographies, autobiographies, chapter books).

* Understands the basic concept of plot (main problem, conflict, resolution, cause and effect).

* Understands similarities and differences within and among literary works from various genres and cultures (in terms of settings, character types, events, points of view, role of natural phenomena).

* Understands elements of character development in literary works (differences between main and minor characters; stereotypical characters as opposed to fully developed characters; changes that characters undergo; the importance of a character's actions, motives, and appearance to plot and theme).

* Makes connections between characters in simple events in a literary work and people and events in his or her own life.

Kendall, J. S. & Marzano, R. J. (2004). *Content knowledge: A compendium of standards and benchmarks for K-12 education.* Aurora, CO: Mid-continent Research for Education and Learning. Online database: http://www.mcrel.org/standards-benchmarks/

References and Additional Resources

Bowman, L. A., Carpenter, J. & Paone, R. (1998). "Using graphic organizers, cooperative learning groups, and higher order thinking skills to improve reading comprehension." M.A. Action Research Project, Saint Xavier University. Chicago, IL.

Boyle, J. R. & Weishaar, M. (1997). "The effects of expert-generated versus student-generated cognitive organizers on the reading comprehension of students with learning disabilities." *Learning Disabilities Research and Practice, 12* (4), 228–235.

Bromley, K., Irwin-De Vitis, L. & Modlo, M. (1995). *Graphic organizers: Visual strategies for active learning.* New York: Scholastic.

Chang, K., Sung, Y. T. & Chen, I. D. (2002). "The effects of concept mapping to enhance text comprehension and summarization." *Journal of Experimental Education, 71* (1), 5–24.

Dodge, J. (2005). *Differentiation in action.* New York: Scholastic.

Egan, M. (1999). "Reflections on effective use of graphic organizers." *Journal of Adolescent and Adult Literacy, 42* (8), 641.

Guastello, E. F. (2000). "Concept mapping effects on science-content comprehension of low-achieving inner-city seventh graders." *Remedial and Special Education, 21*(6), 356.

Jacobson, J. & Raymer, D. (1999). *The big book of reproducible graphic organizers.* New York: Scholastic.

Moore, D. & Readence, J. (1984). "A quantitative and qualitative review of graphic organizer research." *Journal of Educational Research, 78* (1), 11–17.

Pardo, L. S. (2004). "What every teacher needs to know about comprehension." *Reading Teacher, 58* (3), 272–280.

Robb, A. (2003). *40 Graphic organizers that build comprehension during independent reading.* New York: Scholastic.

Skill

✳ Making Personal Connections

✳ Analyzing

✳ Comparing and Contrasting

Management Tip

After modeling how to use this organizer, have students complete it independently and then share their responses during group literature discussions.

Literature Link

Almost Home by Nora Raleigh Baskin (Little, Brown, 2005).

Twelve-year-old Leah has difficulty adjusting to living with her father and stepmother.

That Reminds Me!

Purpose

Students increase comprehension by connecting what they read to their own lives.

Introducing the Activity

Explain to students that actions or events in a story might remind them of experiences in their own lives. Point out that when readers make personal connections to the text, they understand more fully what they read. Then tell students that they will connect events from a book to their own personal experiences.

Using the Graphic Organizer

1. Choose a short story to read aloud to students. Provide copies for students to follow along as you read.

2. As you read, pause when you come to a part of the story that reminds you of an event in your life. Share with students what personal experience came to mind when you read that particular passage.

3. To model how to use the organizer, write a brief description of the story event on the left side of a book. Then write the personal experience that the event reminded you of on the right side.

4. Distribute copies of the organizer for students to complete independently. Have them continue reading the story on their own. Each time they reach a part that reminds them of a personal experience, have them record their connection on a book on the organizer.

Taking It Further

Have students compare the circumstances, setting, emotions, reactions, and so on of the event in the text to their own personal experiences. They might also make text-to-text and text-to-world connections by comparing events to those in other stories they've read or to current world events.

Name _____Mary_____ Date ___April 2___

That Reminds Me!

Title: _____Almost Home_____

When I read this part:
Leah auditioned for the play and was really nervous.

I was reminded of:
This reminded me of the time I tried out for chorus. I squeaked out a few notes, and the director said, "You must have a cold."

When I read this part:
Leah was playing "Little People" with her sister.

I was reminded of:
I remembered playing with my younger cousins and wanting to play with all the toys. Then I realized that I had grown too old for them.

Name _____ Date _____

That Reminds Me!

Title: _____

When I read this part: **I was reminded of:**

When I read this part: **I was reminded of:**

※ Comparing Story Attributes

※ Analyzing Story Elements

※ Making Connections

Literature Link

There Goes Lowell's Party by Esther Hershenhorn (Holiday House, 1998).

Lowell is convinced that not even a brewing storm will spoil his birthday celebration.

Gullywasher Gulch by Marianne Mitchell (Boyds Mills Press, 2002).

All of Eb's junk-collecting "for a rainy day" pays off when flash floods hit Dry Gulch.

Comparing Stories

Purpose

Students compare two examples of literature based on selected attributes, such as setting, character, and plot.

Introducing the Activity

Read two stories aloud, either in tandem or on separate days. The stories may be similar in theme, setting, characterization, or plot. Picture books work well when introducing how to use this graphic organizer to the class.

Using the Graphic Organizer

1. Write each book title in a cloud at the top of the graphic organizer.

2. To model how to complete the organizer, ask: *In what ways are these two stories similar?* Write a few student responses on the large cloud.

3. Choose three attributes that you'd like students to compare in the two stories. You might include attributes such as beginning, ending, setting, characters, plot, theme, tone or style, voice, point of view, or specific events. Write a different attribute on each puddle.

4. Ask students to compare the stories according to the attributes you recorded. Write a response on the umbrella for each story next to each attribute puddle.

5. Distribute copies of the organizer for students to complete independently, comparing two stories they have read.

Taking It Further

Rather than assigning attributes for students to compare, have them leave the puddles blank. Encourage them to record ways in which the two stories are different and then fill in the attributes they used to make their comparisons.

Name _____ Kevin _____   Date __ March 8 __

Comparing Stories

Title: **There Goes Lowell's Party**

Title: **Gullywasher Gulch**

How these stories are similar:

Fun language
Signs of rain

Flooding and muddy waters
Celebrating in the end

Takes place in the Ozark Mountains

Takes place in the desert

Setting

Lowell was afraid rain would wreck his birthday plans.

Ebenezer hoped it would rain more than a spit.

Character

Rain did not ruin Lowell's party!

The town was ruined by the rain and has to be rebuilt.

Plot

Reading Response for Fiction: Graphic Organizers & Mini-Lessons © 2008 by Jennifer Jacobson, Scholastic Teaching Resources, page 11

Name _____ Date _____

Comparing Stories

Title:

Title:

How these stories are similar:

Skill

❋ Visualizing Settings

❋ Drawing Conclusions

❋ Examining Word Choice

Management Tip

To introduce this organizer, have all students use the same word list for a particular setting. Later, they can generate their own lists based on the stories they read.

Literature Link

Love, Ruby Lavender by Deborah Wiles (Gulliver Books, 2005).

Ruby learns to survive on her own in Mississippi by writing letters, making new friends, and finally coming to terms with her grandfather's death.

Name _____ Holly _____ Date ___ Feb. 12 ___

Setting Clues

Title: _____ Love, Ruby Lavender _____

Word Clues

dirt yard   chicken house
egg ranch   split-rail fence
dusty sea   country road
hot June sun   fields

Setting Clues

Purpose

Students list words that describe a story's setting and then draw pictures to show how they visualize the setting.

Introducing the Activity

Ask students: *When you read a story, do you imagine how the characters or setting might look?* Explain that these images are an important part of the reading experience; authors carefully choose words to help readers visualize their stories. Students might also talk about what they visualized as they read a story and how these images matched or differed from a movie version of the story.

Using the Graphic Organizer

1. Read aloud a picture book or passage that contains descriptive words that will help students visualize the setting (don't show any pictures that accompany the passage). Ask them to try to visualize the setting as you read.

2. Distribute copies of the graphic organizer. Have students fill in the title. Then ask them to name words that describe the setting. For example, for *Love, Ruby Lavender* by Deborah Wiles, they might respond with *dirt yard, split-rail fence,* and *country road.* Write the words on the board and have students copy them in the box.

3. Ask students to draw a picture on the camera to show how they visualize the setting based on the word clues list.

4. Invite students to share their drawings. Point out that each person's memory and imagination is unique; although they used the same descriptive words, they most likely drew very different pictures.

Taking It Further

Instead of focusing on setting, have students listen for clues that describe a character and then draw pictures accordingly.

Setting Clues

Title: ————————————————————————————————

Word Clues

Skill

❋ Examining Character Motives
   and Actions

❋ Recognizing Cause-and-Effect
   Relationships

Management Tip

Model how to use this organizer
with the class. Later, have students
complete it independently and then
share their responses in literature
discussion groups.

Literature Link

*Horace and Morris Join the
Chorus (but what about Dolores?)*
by James Howe (Aladdin 2005).

When Dolores doesn't make the
chorus, she writes a persuasive
letter to Moustro Provolone, the
choral director.

What a Character Wants

Purpose

Students examine what a character wants and how he or she tries to
attain it.

Introducing the Activity

Point out that most stories begin with a main character that wants
something. Urge students to think about the main character in their
favorite story (or one they are currently reading). Ask: *What does the main
character want?* You might share these examples:

• Cinderella wants to go to the ball. (*Cinderella*)
• Dorothy wants to go home. (*The Wizard of Oz* by L. Frank Baum)
• Stanley Yelnats wants to leave Camp Greenlake. (*Holes* by Louis Sachar)

Using the Graphic Organizer

1. Choose a picture book to read aloud to students. Then distribute
copies of the graphic organizer. Have students fill in the title.

2. Instruct students to write the main character's name on the line on
the treetop. Then have them write what the character wanted at the
beginning of the story.

3. Ask: *How did this character attempt to get what he or
she wanted?* Have students write the different things
that the character tried on the tree limbs.

4. Invite students to write or draw the story's ending
on the trunk. Ask: *Did the character get what he or
she wanted? Why or why not?*

5. Distribute additional copies of the organizer for
students to complete based on other characters in
the story, or the main character of another story that
they've read.

Taking It Further

Have students use this graphic organizer to plan their
own stories. Explain that their completed organizer will
give them a story outline, but they must provide details
to make their stories interesting.

Name _____ Max _____   Date _ March 4 _

What a Character Wants

Title: ___ Horace and Morris Join the Chorus ___

What _____ Dolores _____ wants:

She wants to join the chorus.

Tries:
Dolores
auditions
but doesn't
make it.

Tries:
She tries to
stop feeling
sorry for
herself by
exploring and
climbing a tree.

Tries:
She writes
a letter
persuading
the
"moustro"
to let
her sing.

And in the end:

Moustro Provolone wants to turn
Dolores' letter into a song. He
agrees that Dolores should be in
the chorus and teaches her to sing.

Reading Response for Fiction: Graphic Organizers & Mini-Lessons © 2008 by Jennifer Jacobson, Scholastic Teaching Resources, page 15

Name _____   Date _____

What a Character Wants

Title: _____

What _____ wants:

Tries: Tries: Tries:

And in the end:

* Making Inferences
* Analyzing Character Traits

Management Tip

After demonstrating how to use this organizer with small groups, have students complete it independently for other books they've read.

Literature Link

Judy Moody by Megan McDonald (Walker Books for Children, 2006).

In spite of her many moods, Judy is pleased when her teacher assigns a "Me" collage project.

Characters That Change

Purpose

Students make inferences about how a character has grown or changed and where this change happens in a story.

Introducing the Activity

Explain that the events of a story often cause growth or change in a character. In E. B. White's *Charlotte's Web*, for example, Wilbur is initially self-centered and consumed by loneliness and fear. But by story's end, he had evolved into a courageous, sociable pig that selflessly saved Charlotte's children. Tell students that the main character usually changes the most, but other characters may also experience change.

Using the Graphic Organizer

1. Read aloud a passage from a book in which the main character experiences a change, such as in *Judy Moody* by Megan McDonald. Ask students to signal each time they hear a part in which the main character has experienced a change. Mark that page with a sticky note and continue reading until you finish the passage.

2. Distribute copies of the graphic organizer. Have students fill in the title and main character's name.

3. Ask students to tell what changes they noted in the character on each marked page. For each incident, have them fill out a row on the chart, noting the page number, the character's change, and evidence to support the change. When finished, discuss students' responses.

4. Ask students to use sticky notes to mark pages on which they note changes in the main character (or another character) of a story that they're reading. Have them complete the organizer and then discuss their responses in small groups.

Taking It Further

Explain that some characters—as in fairy tales or picture books such as Helen Lester's *Tacky the Penguin*—do not change. As they read, encourage students to find evidence that shows that a character has remained constant.

Name _____ Maria _____ Date ___ Jan. 22 ___

Characters That Change

Title: _____ Judy Moody _____

Character	Change	Evidence	Page(s)
Judy	Learns to like Frank	"Judy forgot all about wanting to leave."	110
Judy	Can switch her bad mood with a good one	"She stood tall as her brother had not nearly ruined her masterpiece."	149

Name _____   Date _____

Cause-and-Effect Machine

Title: _____

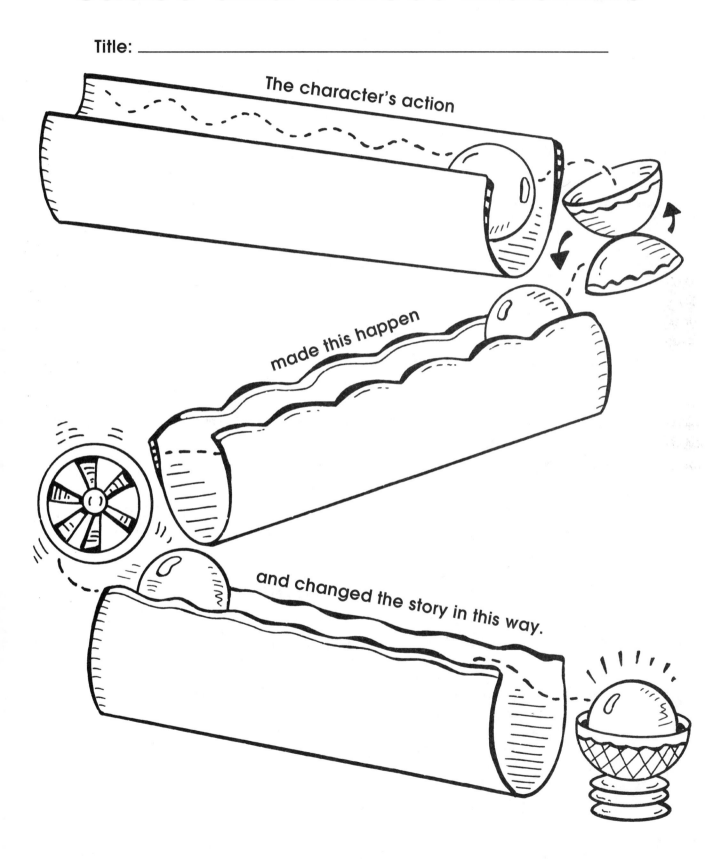

The character's action

made this happen

and changed the story in this way.

Management Tip

Have students complete this organizer in pairs or small groups to encourage discussion and collaboration on determining the plot and subplot of a story.

Literature Link

Holes by Louis Sachar (Yearling, 2003).

Accused of a crime he didn't commit, Stanley Yelnats serves time at a youth labor camp run by an unlawful pair.

Ringing in the Plot

Purpose

Students will identify the plot and subplot in a story.

Introducing the Activity

Tell students that many stories have a plot and one or more subplots. Explain that the plot is the major conflict, while a subplot consists of a minor conflict that connects to the main plot. Often, a subplot introduces new characters and helps readers better understand the story. For example, the plot in *Holes* by Louis Sachar is about Stanley being unfairly sentenced to serve time at Camp Green Lake. One subplot focuses on a family curse; another on his father's quest to eliminate sneaker odor. Each subplot lends depth and humor to the overall plot.

Using the Graphic Organizer

1. Distribute copies of the graphic organizer. Ask students to fill in the title of a story you have recently read. Work with them to identify the plot (or major conflict) and then have them write it on the left side of the board.

2. Discuss key events that lead to the story's conclusion. Have students write three main events in the bells under the plot and the conclusion on the clapper at the bottom.

3. Review the story again with students to determine one or more subplots. Have them choose a subplot to write on the right side of the board.

4. Ask students to write events related to the subplot on the remaining bells and its conclusion on the clapper.

5. Have students complete the organizer for other stories and then share their responses.

Taking It Further

To demonstrate their understanding of how events in the plot and subplot coincide and influence each other, ask students to draw lines to connect the related events on the bells.

Name _____ **Ben** _____   Date __ **Aug. 22** __

Ringing in the Plot

Title: _____ Holes _____

Plot	Subplot
Stanley suspects the warden has a secret reason for having the boys dig holes.	Stanley and Zero become best friends.

Event 1
Stanley is sent to Camp Green Lake as punishment.

Event 1
Stanley helps Zero learn to read and Zero helps Stanley dig holes.

Event 2
He digs holes everyday in the hot, dry sun.

Event 2
Zero runs away from the camp, but gets very sick.

Event 3
Stanley leaves the camp to try to find Zero.

Event 3
The boys climb "God's Thumb" and survive on onions.

Conclusion
The boys find the secret treasure and discover it belongs to Stanley.

Conclusion
Stanley carries Zero down the mountain and breaks the curse.

Reading Response for Fiction: Graphic Organizers & Mini-Lessons © 2008 by Jennifer Jacobson, Scholastic Teaching Resources, page 25

Name _____

Date _____

You're in the Story!

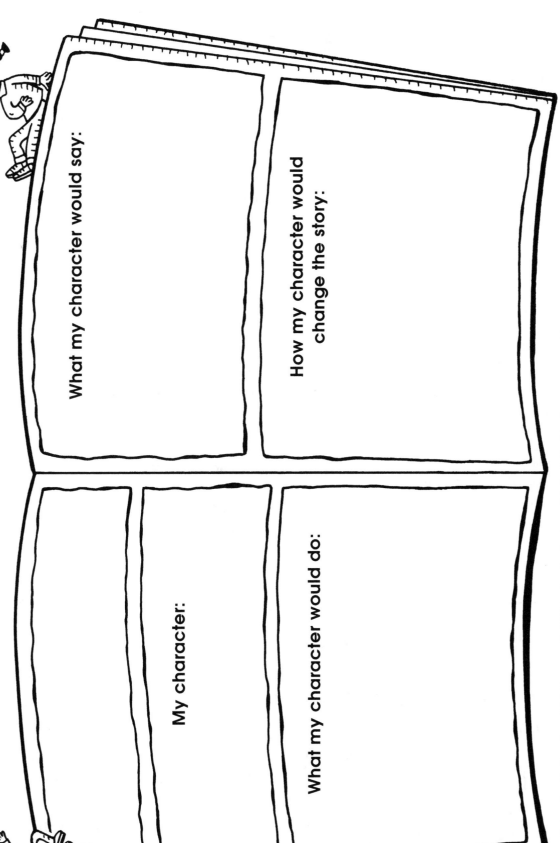

What my character would say:

How my character would change the story:

Title:

My character:

What my character would do:

Reading Response for Fiction: Graphic Organizers & Mini-Lessons © 2008 by Jennifer Jacobson, Scholastic Teaching Resources, page 41

Driving Home the Theme

Purpose

Students use individual words or short phrases to summarize the theme of a reading selection and then give reasons for their choices.

Introducing the Activity

Choose a fairy tale or other familiar story that has one or more themes. Ask students to share words or phrases that come to mind when they think of the message or lesson communicated by the story. For example, they might respond with *friendship, loyalty,* and *determination* to represent the themes conveyed in *Charlotte's Web* by E. B. White. Record student responses on the board, inviting them to tell why they chose those particular words to describe the story's theme(s).

Using the Graphic Organizer

1. Distribute copies of the graphic organizer. Then read aloud a story or selection that conveys a message, or theme. Ask students: *What words come to mind when you think about the theme of what you've just heard?*

2. Ask students to fill in the title of the selection. Then have them write a different word or phrase that describes a message conveyed by the selection on each large window on the car.

3. On each car door, have them write why the word or phrase on the window expresses a theme of the selection.

4. Invite students to share their responses with the class. Remind them that although they all heard the same selection, the message interpreted by each student is personal and might differ from that of classmates.

Taking It Further

Read aloud a poem to students. Have them complete the organizer by writing words on the car windows that describe how the poem made them feel. Then have them write why they felt that way on the car doors.

Name _____Mario_____   Date ___March 13___

Driving Home the Theme

Title: _____Wolf! Wolf!_____

Theme:
Wisdom

Theme:
Be honest

The wolf showed wisdom because he knew the goat would be more useful to him if he kept it alive.

The villagers didn't believe the boy the last time he cried, "Wolf!" This gave the wolf a chance to trick the boy.

Name _____

Date _____

Driving Home the Theme

Title: _____

Theme:

Theme:

Management Tip

Model how to complete this organizer on the overhead projector. Have students fill in their responses on their own copies as you complete each section on the overhead.

Literature Link

Bashful Bob and Doleful Dorinda
by Margaret Atwood (Bloomsbury USA, 2004).

Alliterative text tells the story of two bold, brave friends who work together to find a solution to a serious situation.

Happy Endings

Purpose

Students respond to and interact with a story by examining its ending and considering alternate endings.

Introducing the Activity

Read aloud a fictional picture book such as *Bashful Bob and Doleful Dorinda* by Margaret Atwood. Talk about how the story ends and the events leading to its conclusion.

Using the Graphic Organizer

1. Distribute copies of the graphic organizer. Write the title of the story on the cloud. Have students fill in the title on their copies.

2. On the rainbow, have students write a short description about the story's ending. Then ask: *How do you feel about this ending? Are you satisfied with it? Why or why not?* Encourage students to share their responses with the class.

3. Ask students to consider whether or not they would change the ending if they could. Have them complete the sentence in the top of the pot with "would" or "would not" to indicate their preference.

4. Instruct them to write one or more reasons on the pot to explain their preference for or against the actual story ending.

5. Share and discuss student responses with the class (include your own responses, as well). Invite students to describe any alternate endings they think would work well for the story.

Taking It Further

After completing the organizer, invite students to write their own endings to other stories they have read.

Name _____ Tia _____   Date _____ April 20 _____

Happy Endings

Title:
Bashful Bob and Doleful Dorinda

This is how the story ends:
Bob and Dorinda are reunited with their parents and they all live happily together with their animal friends.

I ___ would ___ change the ending.

Here's why:
I think Bob's parents were too silly to really find him. They might get separated again, so he should just live with Dorinda and the animals.

Name _____

Date _____

Happy Endings

This is how the story ends:

Title:

I _____
change the ending.

Here's why:

Notes: